SALADS

First edition for North America published in 2014
by Barron's Educational Series, Inc.

Copyright © McRae Publishing Ltd 2013 London

All inquiries should be addressed to:
Barron's Educational Series, Inc.
250 Wireless Boulevard
Hauppauge, New York 11788
www.barronseduc.com

Project Director Anne McRae
Art Director Marco Nardi
Photography Brent Parker Jones
Text Edith Bailey
Editing Dale Crawford, Daphne Trotter
Food Styling Lee Blaylock
Food Preparation Mark Hockenhull
Layouts Aurora Granata

ISBN: 978-1-4380-0416-7

Library of Congress Control Number: 2013943556

Printed in China
9 8 7 6 5 4 3 2 1

 Scan and share The QR codes® in this book contain
the ingredients list printed just above them. Easy
and fun to use, they can be scanned by just about
any smartphone or tablet, and the shopping list that pops up
on your display can be forwarded and shared with a friend or
partner at the supermarket, or just stored on your own device
for use when shopping later in the day.

3 EASY STEPS: 1. Download onto your smartphone or tablet a
"QR reader" (a simple App, often available for free); 2. Point
the scanner at the QR code (the 3 black corner squares are
key); 3. The shopping list pops up on your screen.

QR Codes® or Quick Response Codes are a type of barcode.
They were invented in 1994 by and are a trademark of the
Japanese firm Denso Wave, a subsidiary of Toyota, that
granted their free use internationally. Granted patents are
registered with the Patent Offices of Japan, the US, the UK
and Europe.
The use of QR Codes is free of any license.
Granted QR Code patents: US 5726435 (in the USA),
JP 2938338 (in Japan), EPO 0672994 (in the EU).

QR WHAT YOU EAT

SALADS

Edith Bailey

BARRON'S

COUSCOUS-TABBOULEH salad

Serves
4

Preparation
20 min. + 30
min. to stand

Level
Easy

5   tablespoons (75 ml) extra-
    virgin olive oil

1   cup (150 g) fine or
    medium grain couscous

    Salt

2¾ cups (700 ml) boiling
    water

½   cup (120 ml) freshly
    squeezed lemon juice

½   teaspoon ground cumin

1   red bell pepper
    (capsicum), seeded and
    diced

1   pound (500 g) cherry
    tomatoes, halved

1   small cucumber, diced

4   scallions (spring onions),
    thinly sliced

1   cup (50 g) finely chopped
    fresh parsley

¼   cup finely chopped fresh
    mint

    Freshly ground black
    pepper

    Small romaine lettuce
    leaves, for scoops, to
    serve (optional)

Heat 1 tablespoon of oil in a medium saucepan over medium heat. Add the couscous, stir to coat the grains, then cook for 1–2 minutes. Remove from the heat, add ½ teaspoon of salt and 2 cups (500 ml) of boiling water. Shake the pan, cover, and let stand for 7 minutes.

Fluff the couscous with a fork, then pour in the remaining boiling water, half the lemon juice, and the cumin. Cover and let stand for 5 minutes.

Put the couscous in a salad bowl and let cool for 15 minutes.

Add the bell pepper, cherry tomatoes, cucumber, scallions, parsley, and mint, and toss well.

Whisk the remaining 4 tablespoons of oil and the remaining lemon juice in a small bowl. Season with salt and pepper.

Drizzle the dressing over the salad. Serve with the romaine lettuce leaves as scoops, if desired.

This salad is a mixture of the classic Lebanese parsley salad, known as Tabbouleh, with couscous. It makes a satisfying dish that can be served alone or as part of a spread.

Although we think of couscous as a grain, it is actually a type of tiny pasta, made from semolina. It is available in plain and whole-wheat (wholemeal) versions. The whole-wheat version is the more nutritious.

NUTTY coleslaw

Serves
4

Preparation
15 min.

Level
Easy

- 4 cups (200 g) finely shredded white cabbage
- 1 large carrot, coarsely grated
- ⅓ cup (60 g) golden raisins (sultanas)
- 4 scallions (spring onions), finely chopped, white and green parts separate
- 2 tablespoons mayonnaise
- ⅔ cup (150 g) plain yogurt
- 1 teaspoon Dijon mustard
- 1 tablespoon mango chutney

  Freshly ground black pepper
- 6 radishes, thinly sliced
- ½ cup (90 g) salted, roasted peanuts
- 2 tablespoons finely chopped fresh parsley
- 2 tablespoons snipped fresh chives

Mix the cabbage, carrot, golden raisins, and the white parts of the scallions in a large bowl.

Stir the mayonnaise, yogurt, mustard, and mango chutney in a bowl and season with pepper. Stir into the cabbage mixture and toss well to coat.

Just before serving, stir in the radishes and peanuts and sprinkle with the chopped green parts of the scallions, the parsley, and chives.

Packed with vitamins and antioxidants, this coleslaw can be served on its own, or as a side with chicken or fish dishes.

ROASTED VEGGIES with garbanzo beans

Serves
4

Preparation
15 min.

Cooking
30 min.

Level
Easy

1 large red onion, cut into wedges

2 zucchini (courgettes), thickly sliced

2 red bell peppers (capsicums), seeded and cut into large chunks

1 pound (500 g) vine tomatoes

Salt and freshly ground black pepper

6 tablespoons (90 ml) extra-virgin olive oil

Freshly squeezed juice of ½ lemon

2 tablespoons finely chopped fresh parsley

2 (14-ounce/400-g) cans garbanzo beans (chickpeas), drained and rinsed

5 ounces (150 g) feta cheese, crumbled

Preheat the oven to 425°F (220°C/gas 7).

Put the onion, zucchini, bell peppers, and tomatoes in a large shallow roasting pan and season with salt and pepper. Drizzle with 4 tablespoons of oil and toss well. Roast for 30 minutes, stirring halfway through, until the vegetables are tender and beginning to brown.

Whisk the lemon juice and the remaining 2 tablespoons of oil in a small bowl. Season with salt and pepper and stir in the parsley.

When the vegetables are cooked, let cool for 5 minutes, then transfer to a bowl with the garbanzo beans and feta. Drizzle with the dressing, toss gently, and serve.

This is an attractive salad that tastes as good as it looks. You can vary the vegetables according to what you have on hand; eggplant (aubergine), and sweet potatoes would both make tasty additions.

GREEN fattoush

Serves
4–6

Preparation
15 min.

Cooking
5–10 min.

Level
Easy

Salad

1   pound (500 g) fava (broad) beans, fresh or frozen

1   cup (150 g) fresh or frozen peas

1   cucumber

4   pita breads

2   tablespoons coarsely chopped fresh mint

4   tablespoons coarsely chopped fresh parsley

    Small bunch fresh chives, snipped

8   ounces (250 g) feta cheese, crumbled

Dressing

    Finely grated zest and freshly squeezed juice of 1 unwaxed lemon

⅓   cup (90 ml) extra-virgin olive oil

1   teaspoon brown sugar

    Salt and freshly ground black pepper

Salad: Bring a pan of water to a boil, add the beans and peas, and simmer until just tender, 3–4 minutes. Drain well and set aside.

Halve the cucumber lengthwise, scrape out the seeds using a teaspoon, then slice into half-moons. Add to the bean mixture.

Split the pita breads to make eight thin circles of bread, then toast.

Dressing: Whisk the lemon zest and juice, oil, sugar, salt, and pepper in a small bowl.

Pour over the beans and cucumber. Add the mint, parsley, and chives and toss well. Tear the toasted pita bread into pieces and add to the salad with the crumbled feta. Toss gently and serve.

Fattoush is a salad made in many parts of the Eastern Mediterranean. It is based on toasted pita breads which are coarsely torn and mixed with chopped seasonal ingredients.

BLUE CHEESE & BERRY salad

Serves
4–6

Preparation
15 min.

Level
Easy

Dressing

½ cup (120 ml) extra-virgin olive oil

¼ cup (60 ml) balsamic vinegar

1 teaspoon Dijon mustard

Salt and freshly ground black pepper

Salad

4 large slices firm-textured bread

1–2 cloves garlic

3 cups (150 g) arugula (rocket)

2 cups (300 g) strawberries, halved

4 large thin slices prosciutto, torn

8 ounces (250 g) blue cheese, crumbled

Dressing: Whisk the oil, balsamic vinegar, and mustard in a small bowl. Season with salt and pepper, whisking to combine.

Salad: Preheat the oven to 400°F (200°C/gas 6). Toast the bread in the oven until crisp and golden brown. Let cool a little, then run all over with the garlic. Tear into pieces.

Combine the arugula and strawberries in a large bowl. Add the prosciutto, bread, and crumbled blue cheese. Toss gently to combine.

Drizzle with the dressing, toss gently, and serve immediately.

Serve small bowls of this delicious salad as an appetizer before a more substantial course, or pile onto plates and serve as a one-dish lunch. This recipe will serve six as an appetizer and two to four as a one-dish meal.

POTATO SALAD with bacon & blue cheese

Serves
4

Preparation
15 min.

Cooking
40–45 min.

Level
Easy

1 pound (500 g) salad potatoes, halved or quartered, depending on size

Salt

6 tablespoons (90 ml) extra-virgin olive oil

2 red onions, each sliced into 6 wedges

4 slices smoked bacon, rinds removed and cut into large pieces

5 ounces (150 g) mushrooms, sliced

1 tablespoon wholegrain mustard

1 tablespoon red wine vinegar

3 cups (150 g) mixed watercress and spinach salad greens

4 ounces (120 g) blue cheese, such as Roquefort, Gorgonzola, or Danish Blue, crumbled

Preheat the oven to 425°F (220°C/gas 7).

Place the potatoes in a large shallow roasting pan. Season with salt and drizzle with 4 tablespoons of the oil. Roast for 20 minutes.

Add the onions to the pan, stirring gently with a wooden spoon. Roast for 20–25 minutes more, until the potatoes are a deep golden brown and the onions have softened and caramelized. Remove from the oven and let cool slightly.

Meanwhile, heat a large frying pan over medium heat. Dry-fry the bacon until crisp and golden, about 5 minutes. Add the mushrooms and simmer until softened, about 5 minutes.

Whisk the mustard, vinegar, and remaining 2 tablespoons of oil in a bowl until combined.

Put the potatoes, onions, bacon, and mushrooms in a large bowl with the salad greens. Drizzle with the dressing and toss well.

Divide among four serving plates, sprinkle with the blue cheese, and serve.

Serve this nutritious salad as a one-dish meal.

LENTIL & HALLOUMI salad

Serves
4–6

Preparation
20 min.

Cooking
25–30 min.

Level
Medium

1½ cups (280 g) green Le Puy lentils

   Salt

8 ounces (250 g) halloumi cheese, sliced about ½ inch (1 cm) thick

24 cherry tomatoes, halved

1 small red onion, finely chopped

1 clove garlic, finely chopped

3 tablespoons freshly squeezed lemon juice

5 tablespoons (75) extra-virgin olive oil

   Freshly ground black pepper

   Small bunch fresh cilantro (coriander), coarsely chopped

Put the lentils and ½ teaspoon of salt in a medium pot and cover with 6 cups (1.5 liters) of cold water. Bring to a boil, then simmer over low heat until the lentils are tender but not mushy, about 25 minutes.

Remove from the heat, drain, and set aside to cool a little.

Heat a grill pan (griddle) or large frying pan over medium-high heat. Brush the halloumi on both sides with 1 tablespoon of the oil. Add the halloumi to the hot pan and cook until golden brown, 1–2 minutes each side.

Combine the cherry tomatoes, onion, garlic, lemon juice, and remaining oil in a bowl. Add the lentils and toss gently. Season with pepper.

Add the cheese and cilantro, stir gently, and serve.

The small, dark green lentils from Le Puy in France are easily the best type of lentil for salads. Not only do they have a delicious flavor, but they hold their shape well during cooking, and add a wonderful greeny-brown color to the finished dish.

ROASTED BUTTERNUT SQUASH & LENTIL salad

Serves
6

Preparation
20 min.

Cooking
25–30 min.

Level
Medium

Salad

- 4 pounds (2 kg) butternut squash, peeled and cut into 1-inch (2.5-cm) cubes
- 2 tablespoons extra-virgin olive oil
- Salt and freshly ground black pepper
- 1½ cups (280 g) green Le Puy lentils
- 2 cups (100 g) arugula (rocket)
- 1 tablespoon sesame seeds, toasted
- 6 scallions (spring onions), thinly sliced

Dressing

- 5 tablespoons (75 ml) extra-virgin olive oil
- 3 tablespoons balsamic vinegar
- 1 tablespoon soy sauce
- 1 red chili, seeded and finely chopped
- 1 clove garlic, finely chopped
- 1 teaspoon clear honey

Salad: Preheat the oven to 400°F (200°C/gas 6).

Put the squash on a large baking sheet, drizzle with 1 tablespoon of oil and season with salt and pepper. Roast for 20 minutes, until tender, stirring gently with a wooden spoon a couple of times to keep it from sticking.

Put the lentils and ½ teaspoon of salt in a medium pot and cover with 6 cups (1.5 liters) of cold water. Bring to a boil, then simmer over low heat until the lentils are tender but not mushy, about 25 minutes.

Remove from the heat, drain, and set aside to cool a little.

Dressing: Whisk the oil, balsamic vinegar, soy sauce, chili, garlic, and honey in a small bowl.

Put the arugula in a shallow serving bowl and top with the lentils and squash. Drizzle with the dressing, sprinkle with the sesame seeds and scallions, and serve.

Butternut squash, also known as butternut pumpkin, has a sweet, nutty flavor. It comes in winter and is a welcome addition to salads when many other vegetables are out of season.

QUINOA SALAD with zucchini & feta

Serves
4

Preparation
15 min.

Cooking
15 min.

Level
Easy

Salad

1½	cups (280 g) quinoa
2	zucchini (courgettes)
6	scallions (spring onions), thinly sliced
24	cherry tomatoes, halved
1	red chili, seeded and finely chopped
7	ounces (200 g) feta cheese, crumbled
	Small bunch parsley, coarsely chopped

Dressing

⅓	cup (90 ml) extra-virgin olive oil
2	tablespoons red wine vinegar
	Salt and freshly ground black pepper

Salad: Rinse the quinoa in a colander under cold running water. This will remove any traces of the bitter saponin covering that covers these grains.

Put the quinoa in a medium saucepan with 6 cups (1.5 liters) of water. Bring to a boil, then simmer until tender, about 15 minutes. Drain well and set aside to cool.

Cut the ends off the zucchini, then cut lengthwise into long thin ribbons using a potato peeler.

Dressing: Whisk the oil and vinegar in a small bowl. Season with salt and pepper.

Combine the quinoa, zucchini, scallions, cherry tomatoes, chili, feta, and parsley in a large bowl. Drizzle with the dressing, toss gently, and serve.

Quinoa, pronounced "keen-wa," looks like a grain but is actually a member of the grass family. It is gluten-free, making it an ideal food choice for people with gluten intolerance. It is rich in protein, calcium, and iron, and an excellent source of magnesium.

SPICY BEAN salad

Serves
4

Preparation
15 min.

Cooking
7–8 min.

Level
Easy

Salad

4	large eggs
2	avocados, peeled and stoned
2	(14-ounce/400-g) cans red kidney beans
1	red onion, thinly sliced
	Large bunch fresh cilantro (coriander), leaves only, coarsely chopped
25	cherry tomatoes, halved

Dressing

⅓	cup (90 ml) extra-virgin olive oil
2	tablespoons balsamic vinegar
1	red chili, seeded and thinly sliced
1	teaspoon ground cumin
	Salt and freshly ground black pepper
	Toasted tortillas, to serve

Salad: Lower the eggs into boiling water and boil for 7–8 minutes. Place in a bowl of cold water to cool.

Slice the avocados and place in a large bowl with the beans, onion, cilantro, and cherry tomatoes.

Dressing: Whisk the oil, vinegar, chili, cumin, salt, and pepper in a small bowl.

When the eggs are cool enough to handle, peel and cut in half. Add to the salad in the bowl.

Drizzle with the dressing. Toss gently and serve with the tortillas.

GREEK salad

Serves
4

Preparation
15 min.

Level
Easy

Salad

24 cherry tomatoes, halved

1 red onion, thinly sliced

2 cups (100 g) mixed baby salad greens

¼ cup coarsely chopped fresh parsley

¼ cup coarsely chopped fresh mint

8 ounces (250 g) feta cheese, crumbled

20 black olives, preferably kalamata

1 teaspoon finely chopped unwaxed lemon zest

Pita bread, to serve

Dressing

⅓ cup (90 ml) extra-virgin olive oil

Freshly squeezed juice of 1 lemon

Salt and freshly ground black pepper

Salad: Combine the cherry tomatoes, onion, salad greens, parsley, mint, feta, olives, and lemon zest in a large salad bowl. Toss gently.

Dressing: Whisk the oil, lemon juice, salt, and pepper in a small bowl until well mixed.

Drizzle the dressing over the salad and serve with the pita bread.

This is a classic salad that never goes out of fashion.

CANNELLINI SALAD

with roasted tomatoes

Serves
4

Preparation
15 min.

Cooking
20–25 min.

Level
Easy

24 cherry or vine tomatoes, halved

4 tablespoons (60 ml) extra-virgin olive oil

Salt and freshly ground black pepper

5 ounces (150 g) chorizo, sliced and quartered

1 red onion, finely chopped

2 tablespoons sherry vinegar

2 tablespoons honey

2 (14-ounce/400-g) cans cannellini beans, drained and rinsed

2 cups (100 g) arugula (rocket)

Preheat the oven to 350°F (180°C/gas 4). Put the tomatoes on a large baking sheet and drizzle with 2 tablespoons of the oil. Season with salt and pepper and roast for 20 minutes, until softened and almost collapsing.

While the tomatoes are roasting, dry-fry the chorizo in a large frying pan over medium heat until crisp, 3–4 minutes. Drain on paper towels.

Return the pan to medium heat and add the remaining 2 tablespoons of oil and the onion. Season with salt and pepper. Sauté until the onion is softened, 3–4 minutes. Stir in the vinegar and simmer until reduced by half. Add the honey and stir well.

Put the beans in a large salad bowl. Pour the warm onion mixture over the beans, tossing gently. Add the chorizo, cherry tomatoes, and arugula, toss again, and serve.

Cannellini beans are of Italian origin, but are now widely available elsewhere. They are quite closely related to white kidney beans, although they have a firmer texture than kidney beans, making them ideal for salads.

FARFALLE & PESTO salad

Serves
4

Preparation
20 min.

Cooking
15 min.

Level
Easy

Salad

1 pound (500 g) farfalle pasta

¾ cup (180 ml) basil pesto

2 tablespoons balsamic vinegar

½ cup fresh basil leaves

24 cherry tomatoes, halved

8 ounces (250 g) baby bocconcini (mozzarella cheese), halved

Salt and freshly ground black pepper

Pesto

2 cups (100 g) fresh basil leaves

2 cloves garlic, coarsely chopped

½ teaspoon salt

½ cup (60 g) pine nuts, lightly toasted + extra, toasted, to garnish

⅓ cup (50 g) freshly grated Parmesan cheese

½ cup (120 ml) extra-virgin olive oil

Salad: Put a large pot of salted water to boil over high heat. Cook the farfalle in the boiling water until al dente. Drain well and transfer to a large bowl. Shake well to cool a little and set aside.

Pesto: Combine the basil, garlic, and salt in a food processor and blend for 5 seconds. Add the pine nuts, cheese, and half the oil and blend for 5 more seconds. Scrape down the sides, add the remaining oil, and blend until a smooth pesto is formed.

Combine the pesto and balsamic vinegar in a small bowl. Pour over the pasta in the bowl and toss to combine.

Add the basil, cherry tomatoes, and bocconcini. Season with salt and pepper. Toss gently and serve.

This salad is packed with flavor and goodness. If you are pushed for time you may prefer to buy the pesto, although we advise against that since making pesto is so simple and the finished sauce is so much tastier.

EGG & HERB salad

Serves
4

Preparation
15 min.

Cooking
7–8 min.

Level
Easy

8   large eggs

¼   cup finely chopped fresh parsley

¼   cup finely chopped fresh dill

¼   cup finely chopped fresh chives

¼   cup finely chopped fresh tarragon

2   stalks celery, finely chopped

1   small red onion, finely chopped

     Salt and freshly ground black pepper

1   tablespoon white wine vinegar

2   tablespoons freshly squeezed lemon juice

⅓   cup (90 ml) plain yogurt

1   tablespoon mayonnaise

1   clove garlic, finely chopped

1   teaspoon Dijon mustard

2   tablespoons extra-virgin olive oil

4   cups (200 g) baby arugula (rocket)

Lower the eggs into boiling water and boil for 7–8 minutes. Place in a bowl of cold water to cool. When cool enough to handle, shell, and chop coarsely.

Combine the chopped eggs, parsley, dill, chives, tarragon, celery and onion in a large bowl. Season with salt and pepper.

Whisk the vinegar, lemon juice, yogurt, mayonnaise, mustard, and oil in a small bowl. Season with salt and pepper. Toss with the egg mixture.

Line four serving plates or bowls with arugula, top with the egg salad, and serve.

FRENCH BACON & EGG salad

Serves
6

Preparation
15 min.

Cooking
10 min.

Level
Easy

Salad

- 6 cups (300 g) mixed salad greens
- 1 tablespoon finely chopped fresh chives
- 1 red bell pepper (capsicum), seeded and very thinly sliced
- 6 slices baguette (French loaf), toasted, rubbed with garlic, and cut into squares
- 6 large thick slices bacon, rinds removed
- 1 tablespoon vinegar
- 6 large eggs
  Freshly ground black pepper

Dressing

- 2 tablespoons red wine vinegar
- 1 teaspoon balsamic vinegar
  Salt
- 1 teaspoon Dijon mustard
- 1 clove garlic, finely chopped
- ⅓ cup (90 ml) extra-virgin olive oil

Salad: Combine the salad greens, chives, bell pepper, and toasted squares of bread in a large bowl.

Dry-fry the bacon in a large frying pan until crisp and golden brown, about 5 minutes. Drain on paper towels, then cut into thin strips.

Fill a lidded frying pan with water, and bring to a boil. Add the vinegar to the water. Break the eggs into a cup one at a time, then pour from the cup into the pan. Turn off the heat under the pan and cover tightly. Set aside for 4 minutes.

Place a clean cloth next to the pan and, using a slotted spoon, carefully remove the poached eggs from the water. Place on the cloth to drain.

Dressing: Whisk both vinegars, the salt, mustard, garlic, and oil in a small bowl until well combined.

Drizzle the dressing over the salad and toss gently. Divide the salad among six serving plates. Top each one with an egg and some bacon. Season with pepper and serve.

This is a great salad to serve for lunch. You can add more or less bread and bacon, depending on your tastes. You may also like to add some sliced tomato or grated carrot.

WARM SALMON & POTATO

salad

Serves
4

Preparation
20 min.

Cooking
25–30 min.

Level
Medium

2 large red bell peppers (capsicums), halved and seeded

4 tablespoons (60 ml) extra-virgin olive oil + extra, to brush

4 salmon fillets, skin on

3 tablespoons pine nuts

1 pound (500 g) small new potatoes

1 tablespoon balsamic vinegar

3 ounces (90 g) marinated anchovies

2 tablespoons capers, rinsed

½ cup fresh basil, shredded

2 cups (100 g) arugula (rocket)

Preheat the oven to 425°F (220°C/gas 7).

Brush the bell peppers with a little oil, then place, skin-side up, in a large roasting pan. Roast for 15 minutes, then add the salmon to the pan, skin–side down. Sprinkle with the pine nuts and return to the oven for 10 more minutes.

While the bell peppers and salmon are in the oven, boil the potatoes in their skins until tender, 8–10 minutes. Thickly slice or halve, depending on their size.

Whisk the 4 tablespoons of oil with the vinegar in a large bowl. Add the anchovies and capers.

When the peppers are cool enough to handle, peel off the skins, and cut the flesh into long thin strips. Toss in the oil mixture with the basil and potatoes, adding any cooking juices from the baking pan.

Transfer to a large platter with the arugula. Flake the salmon on top in chunky pieces and sprinkle with the roasted pine nuts. Serve warm.

If you don't like anchovies, just leave them out of this tasty salad. It will be just as good.

TUNA & POTATO SALAD

with pesto

Serves
4

Preparation
15 min.

Cooking
8–10 min.

Level
Easy

1½ pounds (750 g) new potatoes, halved if large

1 recipe pesto (see page 28)

8 ounces (250 g) green beans, trimmed and halved

2 cups (100 g) baby spinach leaves

Salt and freshly ground black pepper

12 cherry tomatoes, halved

1 (6-ounce/180-g) can tuna, drained and flaked

Put the potatoes in a pan of lightly salted boiling water, bring back to a boil, then simmer until tender, 8–10 minutes, depending on their size.

Prepare the pesto. Our recipe will make about twice as much as you will need for this salad. Place the rest in a jar and cover; it will keep in the refrigerator for 2–3 days.

Add the green beans to the potatoes for the last 3 minutes of cooking time.

Drain the potatoes and beans, shaking thoroughly in the colander to dry and cool a little. Transfer to a salad bowl.

Stir in the spinach leaves so that they wilt a little from the warmth of the vegetables. Season with salt and pepper. Sprinkle the tomatoes and tuna on top. Drizzle with the pesto, toss gently, and serve.

This salad really is a meal in itself. If you are pressed for time you may prefer to use storebought pesto.

THAI SHRIMP & NOODLE salad

Serves
4–6
Preparation
20 min.
Level
Easy

Dressing

½ red chili, seeded and sliced

1 clove garlic

1 teaspoon brown sugar

   Freshly squeezed juice of 2 limes

1½ teaspoons Thai fish sauce

Salad

12 ounces (350 g) Pad Thai rice noodles

1 small pineapple

3 cups (150 g) bean sprouts

8 ounces (250 g) cooked shrimp (prawns), peeled and deveined

½ cucumber, peeled, seeded, and sliced

20 cherry tomatoes, halved

¼ cup coarsely chopped fresh mint leaves

½ cup (60 g) toasted, salted cashews

Dressing: Mash the chili, garlic, and sugar to a paste with a pestle and mortar. Stir in the lime juice and fish sauce. Set aside.

Salad: Prepare the noodles following the instructions on the package. Drain well and transfer to a large salad bowl.

Peel, quarter, and core the pineapple, then slice into bite-size pieces. Add to the bowl with the noodles, including any juices from the slicing.

Add with bean sprouts, shrimp, cucumber, and tomatoes to the bowl. Toss gently. Top with the mint and cashews. Drizzle with the dressing and serve.

38

You could also use canned pineapple chunks. Make sure they are well drained before adding to the noodles.

SHRIMP & MANGO salad

Serves
4

Preparation
15 min.

Level
Easy

14 ounces (400 g) cooked shrimp (prawns), peeled and deveined

2 mangoes, peeled and sliced

2 small cucumbers, halved and cut into ribbons lengthwise using a potato peeler

1 red chili, seeded and thinly sliced

Large bunch of fresh cilantro (coriander) leaves

Salt and freshly ground black pepper

Freshly squeezed juice of 2 limes

½ cup (120 ml) plain yogurt or sour cream

Warm focaccia fingers or freshly baked bread, to serve

Combine the shrimp, mangoes, cucumber, chili, and cilantro in a salad bowl. Season with salt and pepper. Toss gently.

Whisk the lime juice and yogurt in a small bowl. Divide the salad among four serving bowls .

Drizzle with the yogurt and lime dressing and serve with the focaccia or bread.

Cooked shrimp is widely available in supermarkets everywhere. It will be kept refrigerated. If preferred, you could heat it for this salad by quickly sautéing with a teaspoon of peanut oil in a large frying pan or wok. Don't cook for long, just enough to take the chill off.

SHRIMP & PESTO PASTA salad

Serves
4–6

Preparation
15 min.

Cooking
12 min.

Level
Easy

1	pound (500 g) penne
2	tablespoons extra-virgin olive oil
12	ounces (350 g) peeled cooked shrimp (prawns), peeled and deveined
½	cup (120 ml) pesto, storebought or home-made (see page 28)
3	tablespoons mayonnaise
	Freshly squeezed juice of 1 lime
	Salt and freshly ground black pepper
3	tablespoons finely chopped fresh parsley
2	tablespoons finely chopped fresh basil

Put a large pot of salted water to boil over high heat. Cook the penne in the boiling water until al dente.

Drain the pasta, shaking thoroughly to dry and cool. Place in a large salad bowl. Add the oil and toss gently to coat. Add the shrimp and toss again.

Whisk the pesto, mayonnaise, and lime juice in a small bowl. Season with salt and pepper.

Pour the pesto mixture over the pasta and shrimp and toss to coat. Add the parsley and basil and toss again.

Divide equally among four to six plates or bowls, and serve.

Any short, dried pasta shape, such as fusilli, macaroni, farfalle, ruote, or spirali will go well in this salad. Vary according to what you like or have in the pantry.

CHICKEN & MANGO salad

Serves
4

Preparation
15 min.

Level
Easy

Salad

1	roasted or barbecued chicken
4	cups (200 g) mixed salad greens
2	mangoes, peeled, cut into small cubes
2	avocados, peeled, pitted, and cut into small cubes
½	cup (25 g) fresh cilantro (coriander)
1	long red chili, seeded and thinly sliced
½	cup (60 g) toasted walnuts

Dressing

⅓	cup (90 ml) extra-virgin olive oil
2	tablespoons balsamic vinegar
2	teaspoons Dijon mustard
1–2	teaspoons honey
	Salt and freshly ground black pepper

Salad: Remove the flesh from the chicken. Discard the skin and bones. Shred the chicken flesh.

Combine the chicken flesh, salad greens, mangoes, avocados, cilantro, chili, and walnuts in a large salad bowl.

Dressing: Whisk the oil, vinegar, mustard, and honey in a small bowl. Season with salt and pepper.

Drizzle the dressing over the salad, and serve.

You could roast the chicken yourself, but the easiest solution for this salad is to buy a ready-roasted or grilled chicken at the supermarket.

SPRING CHICKEN salad

Serves
4

Preparation
15 min.

Cooking
2–3 min.

Level
Easy

Salad

1 roasted or barbecued chicken

3 cups (150 g) baby spinach leaves

1 large carrot, peeled, thinly sliced

4 scallions (spring onions), thinly sliced

2 bunches asparagus, trimmed, cut into thirds

3 tablespoons sesame seeds, toasted

Dressing

⅓ cup (90 ml) freshly squeezed orange juice

2 tablespoons tahini

Salt and freshly ground black pepper

Salad: Remove the flesh from the chicken. Discard the skin and bones. Shred the chicken.

Combine the chicken pieces, spinach, carrot, and scallions in a large salad bowl.

Half-fill a frying pan with water. Bring to a boil over medium heat. Add the asparagus. Cook until just tender, 2–3 minutes, depending on the width of the stalks.

Drain well and set aside to cool a little.

Dressing: Whisk the orange juice and tahini in a small bowl. Season with salt and pepper.

Add the asparagus to the chicken mixture. Drizzle with the dressing and toss to combine. Sprinkle with the sesame seeds, and serve.

Another quick and easy chicken salad that can be served as a meal in itself.

LEBANESE CHICKEN salad

Serves
4-6

Preparation
20 min. + 10
min. to soak

Level
Easy

Salad

1   cup (180 g) bulgur

2   cups (500 ml) boiling
    water

1   roasted or barbecued
    chicken

4   ounces (120 g) roasted
    red bell pepper
    (capsicum), from a can or
    jar, drained and thinly
    sliced

1   small red onion, thinly
    sliced

1   (14-ounce/400-g) can
    garbanzo beans
    (chickpeas), drained and
    rinsed

2   cups (100 g) finely
    chopped fresh parsley

1   cup (50 g) finely chopped
    fresh mint

Dressing

¼   cup (60 ml) extra-virgin
    olive oil

⅓   cup (90 ml) freshly
    squeezed lemon juice

    Salt and freshly ground
    black pepper

Salad: Place the bulgur in a heatproof bowl and pour in the boiling water. Stir to combine. Set aside for 10 minutes. Drain well, pressing to remove as much of the liquid as possible. Transfer the bulgur to a large salad bowl.

Remove the flesh from the chicken. Discard the skin and bones. Shred the chicken flesh.

Add the chicken flesh, bell pepper, onion, garbanzo beans, parsley, and mint to the bowl with the bulgur.

Dressing: Whisk the oil and lemon juice in a small bowl. Season with salt and pepper.

Drizzle the dressing over the salad, toss gently, and serve.

This recipe includes bulgur. Remember that it is not the same as cracked wheat; bulgur is made from wheat but has been steamed, dried, and then cracked into grits. Because it is precooked, bulgur only needs soaking, whereas cracked wheat needs cooking. Bulgur is readily available in many supermarkets or in Middle Eastern markets and delis.

GRILLED GREEK CHICKEN salad

Serves
4

Preparation
15 min. + 30
min. to chill

Cooking
5–10 min.

Level
Easy

2	tablespoons plain yogurt
	Freshly squeezed juice of 1 lemon
1	tablespoon dried oregano
2	tablespoons finely chopped fresh mint
1	pound (500 g) chicken tenderloins, trimmed
3	tablespoons extra-virgin olive oil + extra, to drizzle
3	cups (150 g) baby spinach leaves
5	ounces (150 g) roasted yellow bell pepper (capsicum), from a can or jar, drained and sliced
1	cucumber, coarsely chopped
1	cup (50 g) snow pea sprouts
4	ounces (120 g) feta cheese, crumbled
½	cup (50 g) kalamata olives
	Salt and freshly ground black pepper

Combine the yogurt, 2 teaspoons of the lemon juice, oregano, and mint in a bowl, mixing well. Add the chicken, turning to coat. Cover and chill in the refrigerator for 30 minutes.

Preheat a grill pan (griddle), overhead broiler (grill), or barbecue grill on medium heat. Remove the chicken from marinade and brush with the oil. Grill or broil until cooked through, 5–10 minutes, depending on the cooking method.

Combine the spinach, bell pepper, cucumber, snow pea sprouts, feta, and olives in a bowl. Toss to combine.

Divide the salad among four serving plates. Top each portion with a quarter of the chicken. Drizzle with remaining lemon juice and extra oil. Season with salt and pepper, and serve.

If you can't get snow peas, replace them with watercress, arugula (rocket), or another salad green to your liking.

HONEY & MUSTARD chicken salad

Serves
4

Preparation
15 min. + 5
min. to cool

Cooking
5–10 min.

Level
Easy

Salad

4 tablespoons (60 ml) clear honey

2 tablespoons wholegrain mustard

Salt and freshly ground black pepper

4 boneless, skinless chicken breast halves, about 6 ounces (180 g) each

4 cups (200 g) mixed salad greens

20 cherry tomatoes, halved

Dressing

6 tablespoons (90 ml) extra-virgin olive oil

2 tablespoons balsamic vinegar

Salt and freshly ground black pepper

Salad: Whisk the honey and mustard in a small bowl. Season with salt and pepper. Brush all over the chicken breasts.

Preheat a grill pan (griddle), overhead broiler (grill), or barbecue grill on medium heat. Grill or broil the chicken until cooked through and golden, 5–10 minutes, depending on the cooking method.

Let the chicken cool for 5 minutes, then slice.

Combine the salad greens and cherry tomatoes in a bowl. Toss well, then divide equally among four serving plates. Top each portion with a quarter of the chicken.

Dressing: Whisk the oil and balsamic vinegar in a small bowl. Season with salt and pepper. Drizzle over the salads, and serve.

YUMMY DUCK salad

Serves
4–6

Preparation
15 min.

Cooking
15–20 min.

Level
Medium

Salad

1½ pounds (750 g) boneless duck breasts, skin on

Salt and freshly ground black pepper

4 cups (200 g) mixed arugula and watercress salad greens

24 cherry tomatoes, halved

6 scallions (spring onions), sliced diagonally

Dressing

2 cloves garlic, very finely chopped

2 teaspoons finely grated ginger

4 tablespoons (60 ml) soy sauce

6 tablespoons (90 ml) honey

Salad: Preheat the oven to 400°F (200°C/gas 6). Score the skin on the duck breasts and season with salt and pepper.

Heat a large frying pan over high heat. Add the duck, skin-side down, and cook until the skin is crisp, 4–5 minutes. Turn over and brown the underside, then transfer to a baking sheet.

Dressing: Whisk the garlic, ginger, soy sauce, and honey in a small bowl.

Spoon all but 2 tablespoons of the dressing over the duck. Roast the duck until cooked to your liking (10 minutes for pink, longer if you prefer it well done).

Remove the duck from the oven and set aside to rest for 5 minutes. Slice into strips.

Combine the salad greens, cherry tomatoes, scallions, and duck in a salad bowl. Toss gently. Drizzle with the remaining dressing, and serve.

54

Arugula and watercress go very well together and are often sold in mixed bags. If you can't get them both, use one or the other, or other mixed salad greens to your liking.

SWEET POTATO, EGG & CHORIZO salad

Serves
4

Preparation
20 min.

Cooking
15–20 min.

Level
Medium

- 4 large eggs
- 2 large sweet potatoes, skin left on, cut into slices on the diagonal
- 3½ ounces (100 g) chorizo, cut into long slices on the diagonal
- 3 tablespoons extra-virgin olive oil
-   Salt and freshly ground black pepper
- 1 clove garlic, finely chopped
- ¼ cup (60 ml) freshly squeezed lemon juice
- 3 cups (150 g) mixed salad greens
- 20 cherry tomatoes, halved

Put the eggs and potatoes into a saucepan of cold water and bring to a boil. Uncover and simmer for 6 minutes, then lift out the eggs. Place the eggs in a bowl of cold water.

Leave the sweet potatoes in the pan and cook until just tender when pricked in the center with the tip of a knife, about 5 minutes. Drain well and transfer to a salad bowl.

Heat a grill pan (griddle) over medium-high heat until very hot. Toss the sweet potatoes and chorizo in 1 tablespoon of oil and season with salt and pepper.

Grill the sweet potatoes until marked with brown lines, about 2 minutes on each side. Return to the salad bowl.

Peel and quarter the eggs. The yolks will still be a little soft in the center.

Grill the chorizo until crisp and just beginning to release its red oil. Place in the salad bowl, leaving the juices behind.

Remove the pan from the heat, add the garlic and remaining oil, and let sizzle for 30 seconds. Stir in the lemon juice.

Divide the salad greens and cherry tomatoes equally among four serving plates, top with the sweet potatoes, eggs, and chorizo. Drizzle with the hot dressing, and serve.

Choose a good-quality, spicy Spanish chorizo for best results with this salad.

MEDITERRANEAN PASTA salad

Serves
4–6
Preparation
15 min.
Cooking
10–12 min.
Level
Easy

1   pound (500 g) farfalle

2   cups (300 g) frozen peas

1   pound (500 g) tomatoes, peeled

12 sun-dried tomatoes, in oil, drained and coarsely chopped

2   tablespoons extra-virgin olive oil

2   teaspoons white wine vinegar

1   clove garlic

Large handful fresh basil leaves

Salt and freshly ground black pepper

3½ ounces (100 g) thinly sliced prosciutto, torn into large pieces

Put a large pot of salted water to boil over high heat. Cook the farfalle in the boiling water for 8 minutes, then add the peas, return the water to a boil, and cook until the pasta and peas are both done, 2–4 minutes.

Drain the pasta and peas, shaking thoroughly to dry and cool. Place in a large salad bowl.

While the pasta is cooking, chop the tomatoes, half the sun-dried tomatoes, the oil, vinegar, garlic, and half the basil leaves in a food processor until smooth. Season with salt and pepper and chop again briefly.

Pour into the salad bowl with the pasta and peas. Add the remaining sun-dried tomatoes, remaining basil, and the prosciutto. Toss gently and serve.

For a vegetarian version of this dish, leave out the prosciutto and add 4 ounces (120 g) of crumbled feta cheese instead.

GRILLED LAMB & VEGGIE salad

Serves
4

Preparation
15–20 min.

Cooking
15–20 min.

Level
Medium

1   bunch asparagus, trimmed and cut into short lengths

1   cup (150 g) fresh or frozen peas

1   cup (150 g) fresh or frozen fava (broad) beans

6   tablespoons (90 ml) extra-virgin olive oil

1   tablespoon coriander seeds

2   tablespoons red wine vinegar

3   medium salad tomatoes, sliced

     Salt and freshly ground black pepper

     Handful fresh tarragon leaves

     Handful fresh mint leaves

6   large lamb chops

Bring a large pan of lightly salted water to a boil. Add the asparagus, peas, and fava beans. Return to a boil, then simmer until the vegetables are just tender, 2–3 minutes. Drain thoroughly, shaking the colander gently but well to cool and dry. Transfer to a bowl.

Heat the oil and coriander seeds in a small saucepan over medium heat until fragrant, 1–2 minutes. Stir into the vegetables along with the vinegar and tomatoes. Season with salt and pepper, and stir in the tarragon and mint.

Preheat a grill pan (griddle), overhead broiler (grill), or barbecue grill on medium heat. Grill or broil the lamb chops until cooked to your liking, 3–4 minutes on each side for medium-rare, 6–7 minutes for well done.

Place a chop on each of four serving plates and spoon the vegetables over the top. Serve warm.

STEAK & TOMATO salad

Serves
4

Preparation
10 min.

Cooking
15-20 min.

Level
Easy

4	sirloin steaks
2	teaspoons paprika
4	tablespoons (60 ml) extra-virgin olive oil
	Salt and freshly ground black pepper
1	red onion, thinly sliced
30	cherry tomatoes, halved
	Bunch of fresh cilantro (coriander), coarsely chopped
2	tablespoons balsamic vinegar

Rub the steaks on both sides with 1 teaspoon of the paprika and 2 tablespoons of the oil. Season with salt and pepper.

Preheat a grill pan (griddle), overhead broiler (grill), or barbecue grill on medium heat. Grill or broil the steaks until cooked to your liking, 3–4 minutes on each side for medium-rare, 6–7 minutes for well done.

Remove from the heat and let rest for 5 minutes before slicing into strips.

Combine the onion, cherry tomatoes, cilantro, remaining paprika, and remaining 2 tablespoons of oil and vinegar in a bowl. Season with salt and pepper.

Toss the salad gently with the sliced steak, and serve warm.

This is a complete meal. It is ideal for those following a low-carb diet.

INDEX